DEVOURED

poetry for shattered hearts

A.X. SALVO

ABOUT THE AUTHOR

A.X. Salvo is the author of the international bestselling poetry collections *The Teeth Of The World Are Sharp,* *The Muse Of Love & Pain*, **and** *Devoured.*

Salvo's writings and art have appeared in *USA Today,* *MISC, Studio Visit Magazine, Bete Noir, The Adroit Journal*, **and** *The Anthologist.* **Salvo is also the recipient of a Vermont Studio Center grant for Poetry**.

www.axsalvo.com
Instagram: axsalvo

DEVOURED

CONTENTS

DEVOURED: ACT ONE

DEVOURED: ACT TWO

DEVOURED: ACT THREE

I want to be alone and I want people to notice me — both at the same time.

Thom Yorke

I dedicate this book to every woman who has shown the patience to love me, the strength to help me, and the wisdom to leave me.

DEVOURED: ACT ONE

**LOOKING
FOR WARM PLACES
IN COLD PEOPLE**

Someone once asked me what I want out of life. Without hesitation I said: I just want to stay in my little cottage all day and write and paint and drink coffee and wine and make love. Is that too much to ask? I think not.

THE RED ROOM

I've found myself,

my eyes,

lingering over your photographs

imagining how your laugh

lilts and sings

or how it would feel to run

my fingers over

your lips and limbs

I have dreamt of hiding

from my life

from the world

in a dim red room

with you beside me

listening to your

voice bend

vowels in the dark

SELFISH

I'll never

shake

the shame

of keeping you

all to myself

NOTHING

Once you looked upon me

with the eyes of an architect

wanting nothing

but to build great things

your eyes are now

filled with arson

wanting nothing

but to watch

my face burn

NO TIME FOR CONVERSATION

I

I just want to be used

no time for conversation

I don't need a friend now

I need a lover

One

Brutal

Lover

This has nothing

to do with love

or friendship

or even lust

this is about

absolving my sins

with your skin

this is about me

burying my guilt

deeper and deeper within you

(each thrust deeper than the last)

I want you to force

your tongue past

closed angry lips

choke me until I'm blue

slap me until I'm red

ride me till my eyes

go pearl white, bite

me until I bleed, scratch

into the flesh of my back with

scarlet fingernails, lick

the length of my collar bone

. . .

I want to be left

with bruises everywhere

my face, neck, chest,

thighs and cock, I want you

to grab fists full of

my long coffee-brown hair and

pull and pull and pull

until I'm forced to yell

moan

squeal

cry

II

I've taken

beatings before

I've given

a fair share of them myself

I can take

all kinds of punishment: I've been

punched, choked, stabbed and

burned and kicked and pushed

face to the piss-and-shit-wet-ground and

I have scars

some muddy some clean

that would welcome more

This transaction

would cost

nothing

III

Can you please

mistreat me?

This life has grown

tiresome

I just need a little

abuse before bed, it helps

me sleep, you know

And when you're finished

turn off the heat

turn off the lights

take all the blankets

when you leave me

lavender

bare

frigid

tattered

in that topaz darkness

Because this

will always be about

the benefits of frustration

self-loathing, and a little

abuse

these are my burdens

these are my faults

this is my mess

never yours

TREES AND DEMONS

Shake my tree of life and

watch the serpents fall

rearrange me until I'm saved

until I'm safe

consider this a plea for help

turn this demon into a saint

paint my red sins white

paint my black soul blue

teach me the algorithms

to life and love

for I know nothing of either

KEEP ME

Thinking of you

is one of the few things

that keep me anchored to this life

There is something there

something in the ether between us

A signal towards

something good

something more

than sexual

than friendship

Something necessary

necessary to keep

the blood in motion

and the mind at ease

Possibly even,

a more important thing

than love

Keeping me

from death

FLOWERS AND BULLETS

Eyes
disarming

Eyes
like weapons

Every emotion
all at once

Blooming

Blooming
from her eyes

A MUSE GLOWS IN BROOKLYN

There was something about you

about your canine grin and

the way that black dress

wrapped around your

cellophane skin

How you weren't bothered by

my crooked smile or

my wrinkled brow or

my shallow breath and

bourbon stench

I wondered

about the fact that you had

flames for fingertips

yet it never hurt when you

traced the lines of my face

I wondered:

what the hell

such a creature of myth

was doing in a dive like this?

I wondered:

could you replace my

Thorazine?

could you soothe me better than

Cezanne?

Could we help

each other?

Sure, you had your doubts

but that was before

Before I gave my speech:

. . .

Oh yes...

our needs may be

too heavy,

our chests may be

too empty,

but

we have things in common

don't we?

We both drink whiskey

neat

and understand Kandinsky

We both like

the way I grab your ass

the particular texture

of my calloused hands

But I'm too old

too old for you

that's what they'll say

this is a matter

of not if, but when

you'll pull away

Find a younger,

leaner, cleaner, less hopeless

version of me

But just for tonight

Can I leave with you?

TOUCH

Tonight

No amount of liquor
can bring me love

No amount of love
can intoxicate me

And
not even
the touch of tree bark
can make me feel a part
of this world

DIRT

I can already feel

the dirt of yesterday's

disappointment

soiling my today

I'm beginning to feel like

everyone's whore

Worst part being

I'm the one

paying for everything

ENDLESS

We were

fear and flesh and hope

thirsty and tired and alive

sadness and darkness and laughter

dreamcatchers and love-makers

and sweet-talkers

explosive and ferocious and quiet

mismatched, but somehow perfect

We were...

We are...

Everything and nothing

· · ·

And these are

Our

Endless

Numbered

Days

PULP FICTION

Bury me

in your breasts

hold me hostage

at the edge

of your spindle tongue

I find shelter here

and here alone

from voices

so loud they blind

Wrap my neck

in a near choke

to be

smothered by your

arms and skin and scars

I am pulp

I am squeezed

I am shaped

by your needs

NURSE HALO

My Miracle

comes to me at dusk

when I am most weak

whispering words of comfort

coloring this violet silence

with her golden hues

warmth in this wide, windy place

My Miracle

hums in gentle notes

imparting calm on an impatient man

a welcome interruption

to this soliloquy

her sweet song fills my cold lungs

with melody

My Miracle

devours the darkness with desire

turning devils to sand

she divides the surface of my mind

and searches for fissures to repair

My Miracle

cleanses me

she bathes me

in a ritual of

milk

honey

and dream

My Miracle

shows me the way

lighting the caverns to

solace with love

plentiful

with flesh

with sex

with clasped hands

I am finally beautiful

I am wealthy

in lust

in adoration

in admiration

of this Miracle

And so I wait...until dusk

LILY

Her first sight of snow

the pitch black grief

in her eyes

merciless and unwavering

Whales, stars, and soft pastels

buffalo wings and fries

too drunk too fast

running into trees

Small green houses with

small ash white roofs

beautifully small and

beautifully meek features

colored soft gold

with morning sun

To inspire her laughter

every short day

was to triumph again and again

We should have married

at first light

at first fucking light

before time had a chance to pull us apart

to tear away

to ruin

Sickness

Survival

Her grief, then my grief,

now our grief

Waking and haunted

asleep and haunted

plain white pills

There is no escape

ice melts slow here

love grows fast

Please come back

Please come home

Love

awful, awful love

Turn off the lights

DECEMBER

Today, all I could think of

was that December night

How we,

drunk and stumbling,

were figuring our way back

out the back of that dive bar

cutting through

the dim space between

the old gray church

and the crowd of leafless trees

You fell into a patch

of snow and branches

hurt your arm and knees

I scooped you up

from the ground

held you steady and said,

It's O.K. We're almost there

And with no need

for star light

or street lamps

I helped you

find your way home

And that's all I ever wanted,

to hold you steady

and help you find home

DEVOURED: ACT TWO

**AND STILL,
I CLING**

Why must there be a reason to be drunk? Why must there always be something to grieve or celebrate? Why can't we drink merely for the sake of getting drunk? To slow things down. To feel. To live. To ease into the night like we ease into our lovers.

DROWNING

Will you meet me

at the bottom of the ocean?

The currents your hands make

reach me before

your fingers reach the

flesh of my face

before your lips land

on my eyes and

bring the world into focus

This consolation, however brief,

is the light that warms this abyss

that divides the

shadow from the good

This love is what binds

the wolf to the tree, what

quiets those apparitions of guilt

the deafening ghosts' cry

What a fool I've been

living life, believing I could win

this war at my core

this search for epiphany, meaning

in a world whose language

I can speak

but will never understand

My past still

clings to my skin, the stink

I cannot wash, but may

one day purge with

your milk, your nourishment

At the bottom, perhaps

we will find a little peace

the quiet we seek

with every breath

Until then, I ask and ask and

fling my questions into the abyss

waiting for the moment

my destiny is revealed

What will galvanize my being?

What will be the catalyst

that will make my self implode?

Revealing a better structure

a less flawed edifice

a man deserving of

a great woman

Is this hope valid,

or will my sins find me here?

reach me here?

These fears

cut my courage

into slivers, and I

can do nothing but wait

with you at my side

cradling my face

in your small hands

at the bottom of the ocean

HURT

Without you
I am weightless

Without you
my mouth
is dry and hungry
as a withered beggar

Without you
my mind
is madness
my passion
dissolved

. . .

These thoughts

are injuries

I cannot sustain

4 AM

A man can

only go so

long without a lover

Sadness will make him mad

Madness will make him sadder still

And above all

this

remains clear

I

do not belong here

JANUARY AFTERGLOW

Sunday morning

colors our modest bedroom

I study the little yellow strands of light

as they dance across your flesh

A gentle, decadent waltz

across your snowy streets and hills

Apprehensive and still,

thinking of our night in this afterglow

I'm eager for your awakening

Your bare, suspended porcelain

wanting for

my particular touch

My rough hands explore

your glowing features

lips embrace in an incandescent kiss

limbs and souls intertwine and merge

The unified rhythm of

unified bodies

Music

Sweet, sinful song composed by

star-crossed, naïve lovers

believing we were alone

on a great blue spinning sphere

in that pocket of time

that fierce blaze of heat

sweat and heavy breath

that iridescent storm

of sexual bliss

. . .

We visited

a kingdom close to Eden

and passed our own fate

our own deaths

immortalized as brilliant vessels

for love

wisdom

truth

and poetry

WHERE THE RIVER MEETS
THE SEA

No longer alone

we smile

we bend

we moan

such desperate shadows

tinted red

double exposure

in a small dark room

This is how we atone

for all the wrong

we've done

to ourselves

. . .

Sometimes,

it's the only way

to keep our demons dormant

and fill that eternal cavity

for just one somber moment

How else

will we endure

the night?

Estuary

Estuary

We stagger

through our deaths

through memories

of all the things that made us

hurt, shiver, laugh and howl

We are all rivers

We are all oceans

We whisper to each other

like nervous prisoners with

separate cells

yet, always

united somehow

Many have taken their bites

but only you

were willing to swallow me

whole

MELODY

Free me of this guilt

with a passing of the hands

across my face and skin

slow the crescendo of my wickedness

with a sultry kiss

Exhume the strength that fueled

my passion for living, after such a

long period of forgetting

remind me of my admirable qualities

with your exhibitions of

kindness, sincerity, and sanctity

. . .

Murder every demon

inside me

with only your voice

the music

that composes me

LUST JUNKIES

I

A girl once left me

with many

marks, cuts, and bruises

her emerald eyes were always

hard and petulant just as

the life and mind of a

recovering addict should be

She took it all

out on me, gave me

all the rage

she could summon

. . .

She wrapped tattooed palms around

my lithe strained neck

shoved elbows into the blades

of my shoulders

force fed me

bare breasts

bony limbs

smoky lips

and a pierced

fuchsia clit

II

After I finally tore

free from her hold, I

buried my shovel into her soil, I

proved I was

just as guilty

just as shameless

just as vicious

I dug and dug and dug and dug

daring, desperate and dying

to find something underneath the girl

underneath me

She wailed and made a scene of it

an outpour of wicked pleasure

she whispered: I'm crying

because it feels too good

but I knew she cried

because she thought

she didn't deserve to feel good

because there's no such thing

as feeling too good

III

She'd always say:

how her thighs were too thick

her lips too thin

freckles too many

voice too small

eyes too shy

and I always

proved her wrong

She cut crimson diagonals

over the skin of my ribs

with dirty crooked nails

gripped me with a

violence leaving

violet fingerprint phantoms

over the translucent flesh of my waist

(That emblazoned trail of

the narcotic bliss we felt)

Another high

tugging on our blue cables

filling us with the promise

of a momentary fix

Lust junkies

pallid and livid

always looking for the back door

always coming down

slippery steps

Moans became whimpers

we had hurt each other

somehow

I had gone too far

inside her

risked too much

beside her

just to hide our rage - our grief

somehow

DEEP GREEN

Oh, I beg you

can I follow?

You're my fever

running high

running deep

running wild

And across the river

at the pier

in the twilight

your beauty glows

sad, glorious, and

in full bloom

like a vast orange grove

engulfed in flame

And after midnight

when your madness

bursts into full bloom

and you unravel like a

starling lost in a storm

I'll follow...

I'll follow...

I'll follow you

down into the ocean

I will gladly leap

once again

into that same

Cold

Dark

. . .

Deep

Green

WHERE YOU SLEEP

I

I lost you

in a forest of blue-green

flames

I don't know

how to find you

So many years have passed

since you've visited

I remember the raw

umber of your eyes,

but not the shape

. . .

I remember the angry

red of your hair,

but not the smell

I remember the quiet

pink of your mouth,

but not the laughter

I remember the bloodless

white of your skin,

but not the taste

Try as I might,

I no longer

dream of you.

I lost

my place again,

my home again,

my friend again

And now,

only Death and Death alone knows

who looks after you and

where you sleep

II

But I know where and

how your tomb lies

how quiet the black earth has become

I don't regret

ignoring your grave

all these years

it doesn't matter

where we buried you

you were never here

Death is stubborn -

she refuses to take me

to your bedside

until I satisfy

needs and deeds

unknown

Until then,

I will do my best

to keep these unsteady hands

and their wanting

for the golden dagger

that will bring me

back

to you

GOOD

I wondered of

how many men you've left

marooned

on fruitless islands

I cried until

my tears turned

the dirt

beneath my feet

into mud and charred

antlered devils

with maroon skins

burst through the ground

to slather us (our sex)

with soil and love and smut

Sin never felt

so goddamned good

ABSENCE

Your presence

made such

a deep impression

on me that

your absence

has left me

cavernous

NOISE

I thought

you were sent to

soothe a smoldered soul

I thought

you understood

I'm translucent and fragile

as rice paper

You treated my bones

like the branches

you tread upon

when you stepped away

from our home

and into that seething sun

Now

I do nothing, but

sleep and dream

sleep and dream

sleep and

dream guillotine dreams

To sever myself

from this mind and its

severe thoughts with

One

Quick

Cut

Asleep, yet awake

running, yet still

I burn

without flame

whispers are now screams

everything is noise

PAPER DOLLS

Should we darken this ocean?
Should we call it a night?

Let's put on our best clothes
with these paper hands
my black suit, black hat
your sequin dress

I part my dark brown locks
like a mad man
you tie your yellow strands
tight above
your manicured brows and
kale colored eyes, place

the white handkerchief

in my pocket

We each smile

small smiles

We dance, you spin

from black sanded shore

to soft lit sea

warm salty water rushes into

our glossy new

leather shoes

With hands clasped

we love but care

for nothing

Today

we escape

we escape

Our bodies pulled

toward a bright, nude moon

. . .

We run deep, deep

deep into a most

unwholesome darkness

with such sick desperation

hoping

the tide

won't reject us

INFINITE

My universe

grew

with every word

you spoke

DEVOURED: ACT THREE

**WHERE I END
AND YOU BEGIN**

I'm always either ablaze with passion or frigid as a corpse. But once that fire is lit, I keep chasing it madly until it goes out completely. Until everything goes dark and cold again. It's my nature. And it always will be.

GHOSTS

It's so strange

isn't it?

How people appear

and vanish

from our lives?

THE SMALL THINGS I DO

I am surrounded

in a crowded Manhattan pub

full of single souls

with their bright teeth and

trim shapes and long legs

To hell with them

I'm in the corner, slung over

a wooden stool, avoiding

all conversation

The women here stare at me

their eyes say

they want to touch me,

but I don't want their hands

I need yours

I don't want anyone

to touch me but you

So I drink and

fool myself into forgetting

Desperate to find a way to bury you

I search my mind for the shovel

I distract it, seeking redemption in

the small things I do

I throw colors against a canvas

I water my plants

I conjure a poem

call my father

check my email

beat my face

into the bathroom tiles

iron pants

I will never wear

jerk my cock

bite my nails

drink coffee

sweep the floor

argue with a cashier

walk through the bad

parts of town after dark

drink whiskey

jerk my cock

drink more whiskey

listen to Radiohead

fight strangers

weep with

all the lights off

Sleep

But it's not enough

It never is

LOVE IS...

feeling immortal after a kiss

completion

agony when she is away

laughing at her jokes when

they are far from funny

staring at her scarlet lips for hours

crying when she is in pain

the blood in her veins

never tiring of her madness

hanging on her every syllable

yearning to taste her voice

the color of her skin

the confused strands of her hair

the division of light

when she enters a room

redemption

healing with only her touch

waiting for our time to slow

the moment

her arms close around me

rain down her face

her smile that can

melt steel and stone

talking for hours without pause

lightning through me

as she calls my name

always smelling her perfume

wishing to love her, yet

never able to

SWEET FIRE

Red hair drapes

over me

over my entirety

stretching

caressing

surrounding me

wrapping

spidering around my

grinning face

closed eyes

bare throat and

restless heart

A strawberry-blonde gossamer

befalls and enthralls my bones

as I spread my trembling, wet lips

over yours

My darling, dying valentine

my beautiful, burning shadow bride

give me life

THIS IS FOR YOU (ANOTHER YOU)

I'd give a rib to make another you

I'd break another bone

I'd beat another man

I'd do that too

I'd set fire to cities

I'd blacken pale angels

I'd deal with the Devil

I'd do that too

I'd carve myself another face

I'd wrap myself in wire

I'd make myself expire

I'd do that too

If it would bring us closer

Make me closer

To another you

PINK

I saw your lips

and my imagination trailed

Your lips were projected

onto the walls of my mind

and I understood them

to be not unlike

two great feathery

pink clouds pressed

against the sky

NOT THIS LOVE

May this love

be durable and sound

may it also be violent

and never flinch

when confronted by floods

of adverse circumstance and

droughts of good days

Many mountains and tall trees

lie in our path

this place has many obstacles

Devils beg for our attention

at each crossing

daggers clutched behind their backs

Men scheme with malicious intent

peril awaits us

But never allow

your strength to be compromised

never allow

your will to be tampered

You did not allow your wounds

to slow your journey forward

towards love and now

it is here

it is present

it is omnipotent

Find solace in this essential truth

remember this if nothing else

wear it around your neck as you would

a woolen scarf

for protection

from the inevitable cold

I question God, government, and the

behaviors of man,

but not this love

no, not this love

YOU DESERVE IT

Don't be shy

Scoot
a bit closer, dear

Let's escape
to the rooftop

Talk about
everything and nothing
and fire up
incense and cigarettes

Reveal

our dark faces

without remorse

Listen to

a lark named Yorke

croon till sun up

Read

our poetry aloud

without fear, and revere

the fact that

despite it all,

we're still here

Have a drink with me...

you deserve it

WILL

Having gone so long

without your sound

without your fury

It's as if

you've died

and

I am unsure if

I can continue

to exist

in a world where

you do not

. . .

But I will try

my love

I

will

try

DEVOUR

Much like the

blood red berries

that stained the

skin of your

pale and perfect fingers

I nourish you as

you devour me

FICTION

Thank you

for reminding me

that I exist

That when I speak,

I am heard

That when I weep,

I am heard

That when I whimper in pain,

I am held

That you will wake me

when my nightmares

become more than

fiction

WARM MACHINES

I

Sifting through the wreckage,

the tousled stranger

finds wire

finds metals

finds threads

of light

fine ovals

of shadow

stitches, staples, tape

bolts, batteries, clay

Forms

a man

forms

a woman

We are

such

warm machines

such

warm machines

II

We wake

shin skin torn

our shells devastated and muddy

covered in night

in a field of blood-

orange leaves

Our blue metal is starting to show

everyone will soon get suspicious

we may have to start

running soon

furious as exposed spies

I stare at the sky

I say:

those stars don't look

quite right tonight

eyes glimmer and do not

merely watch

they whisper

the darkness purrs

I plead:

we should go away for a while,

my love

but you never listen

III

You look beyond the field

at the hanging garden

impressed by

the strange animals

filling and drinking

their bejeweled cups of wine

surrounded by

great, gray stone pillars

.   .   .

I pull at you and say:

this is nothing but theater

this is no Babylon

You look out

at the silent animals

to find

a crowd

of smiling still

faces like foxes,

bodies of angels

clothed in the coldest light

and fire

questions

Why can't I do that?

what is happiness?

why can't I be like them?

how long must we wait?

when

will we be like them?

and after

a long stretch of quiet

I say:

never

We're just

warm machines

such

warm machines

We will never

eat how they eat

speak how they speak

think how they think

breathe how they breathe

love how they love

fuck how they fuck

That's why you sleep

and can't stand

to be around

too many

of them for

too long

. . .

Why you rarely leave

this field of dead red leaves

Because

ours,

ours is

a colder kind of love

a stranger spell of magic

a warmer form of logic

ruled by zeros and ones

and not

the constant threat

of oblivion

we cannot understand

fear

Death does not shake us

funerals are not events

We can never die

because

we were never truly alive

. . .

We're just

warm machines

such

warm machines

IV

I,

I am an inferior model

made of plastic and copper and tin

living barely on oil and coal

You,

you are awakened by and filled with

the sun

you are

made of gold and light and porcelain

I

I am

built from parts

used and mislabeled -

something is off

on

the inside

there are pieces missing

Can't you tell this by my gait?

(every move I make

sounds like

loose change

spilling 'round the bottom

of a bucket)

Made listless,

I'll still manage

love

somehow

I cannot bruise,

but I will bend and

most certainly rust

time is a

hell of a thing,

my love

V

Those goddamned animals,

you'd think

they would know better

than to come here

than to

touch

our crimson wires

linked to the

chambers

of hearts imperfect

Those goddamned animals

and their curious hands

We explode

blown back

into the hanging garden

We run

they chase

pull us apart

try to learn

what made us undead

try to steal

what keeps us awake

But

we use what we've learned

patterns, rhythms, algorithms

we use what we've learned

to survive, to live

but only as fugitives

(repeat after them)

If you say this

they'll believe that

Assimilated

we convince them that we are

one and the same and

for a moment

we find safety

in numbers

VI

Once

during your absence

someone touched

the wrong wire

a careless error

system corruption

severed connection

broken transmission

loss of communication

blank screens

phantom dreams

flickering imagery

My screams

became

your screams

a lifetime of nothing

became everything

we never wanted

Snow snuck into our lives

winter hid all the places

we found ourselves

. . .

Tongues were held

gradually

more than hands

No longer able to

process your affection

I finally recognize

how obsolete I've become

You say:

Don't you leave me here

Don't you want to find

where you belong?

Don't you want to find home?

With my back to you, I

face the distant wreckage

and say:

My love,

I have found home

. . .

You say:

Don't you dare leave me here

I stare

at the ravens above the wreckage

and say:

If I don't go now

someone will just

come and take me away

any way

I may never know

what manner of science or religion

governed his or her or its vision

But of this,

I am certain

If this is my end

and

you cannot go on

without me

. . .

Whoever

created us

made

two

terrible

mistakes

THE BEDROOM

I entered the bedroom

and envisioned her asleep

under the cream colored blanket

the swirled black and gray patterns

mimicking the slopes and shapes

of her hips and legs

I had lost count of how many times

I marveled at her glow and thought:

My God, she is beautiful

I thought of the pleasant

inviting gray of her eyes

how they always seemed to

calm my anxious brain with

a sincere sense of hope

For years, I had avoided

people's gaze

but there I was, perfectly

at ease in the stare

of a lovely stranger

I pressed my face against

her pillow and inhaled

her scent

I stumbled back

and covered my mouth

with my hand

to stifle the grief

It was futile

the pain always

clawed its way out

The tears were inevitable:

she was gone

. . .

She achieved a miracle:

my happiness

I felt a wonderful thing –

that bitterness in my chest

beginning to thaw

This was the dark space

in which we made love

This is where

I taught her how

unique she truly was

How the origin of her sadness

was rooted

in the fact that this world

wasn't good enough for her

That much like myself,

she was an alien

meant for elsewhere

.   .   .

I hope, in time, she'll realize

true love and liberty

and in these realms –

her true potential

The bedroom was where

she stopped suffocating

where she breathed

deep and relaxed and learned

how beautiful it is

to have your lungs

filled with passion

Passion for flesh and friction

and honesty and poetry

and all the small things

that one remembered

long after a long night

with a close lover

The bedroom: *it was our place*

where

no one could touch us

no one could harm us

We were safe

from a world

that never wanted us

We didn't

belong here,

but we could

belong to each other

and that was enough

AFTERWORD

THANK YOU for taking the time to read my words and supporting my work! When you purchased this book, you made one strange little indie artist extremely happy!

If you enjoyed **DEVOURED**, please take a moment to rate the book on Amazon and/or Goodreads.

Explore my other books.

The Teeth Of The World Are Sharp
An illustrated collection of dark art and poetry inspired by Edgar Allan Poe, Sylvia Plath, Neil Gaiman and the horror manga of Junji Ito. *The Teeth Of The World Are Sharp* explores trauma, abuse, death, grief, and loss. Each poem is carefully illustrated with haunting black and white drawings

Where I End And You Begin
In this fourth collection of poems, Salvo takes you deeper into the shadows and delivers another brutally emotional experience with even more of what readers loved from his bestselling book *The Teeth Of The World Are Sharp* with more than 150 pages of new poems and

hauntingly beautiful black and white drawings that blend dark fantasy, myth, and horror.

Beautiful Shadows
An illustrated anthology of dark art and classical poetry that includes famous poems by Poe, Neruda, Frost, Keats, and many others!

The Muse Of Love & Pain
Blurring the lines of poetry and fiction, this blend of gothic verse and fable is an ode to anyone who has traveled through the darkest roads and deepest waters to find love.

Pretty Hate Machine
A macabre horror/sci-fi tale told from the monster's perspective. *Pretty Hate Machine* introduces us to the trials of Orion. The ruthless beast that stalks the streets of the dystopian Chaoxte in search of human prey.

CONTINUE THE BEAUTIFUL SHADOWS POETRY SERIES!

CUT

Now I kneel here

at her grave

wondering

which words to say

I sensed this loss

so long before

that sad, slow knock

came at my door

Now I lay here

in the snow

shaking

naked

and alone

I'll cut myself

and bare my bones

until I see

her perfect ghost

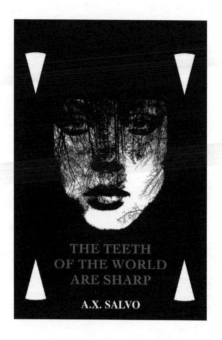

KEEP READING THE TEETH OF THE WORLD ARE SHARP

"I have never seen a more hauntingly beautiful book. It is a wonderful collection of poems and art that cuts deep from a place of tragedy and love."

AVAILABLE NOW IN PAPERBACK AND E-BOOK

Made in the USA
Columbia, SC
19 August 2021

43945259R00086